Voices Yearning

PALMETTO
PUBLISHING
Charleston, SC
www.PalmettoPublishing.com

Copyright © 2024 by Douglas Gordon Magid

www.voicesyearning@gmail.com

First paperback edition June 2024

Book cover design by
@jooneydraza (Fiverr)

All rights reserved

No portion of this book may be reproduced, stored in a retrieval system, or transmitted in any form by any means–electronic, mechanical, photocopy, recording, or other–except for brief quotations in printed reviews, without prior permission of the author.

Paperback ISBN: 979-8-8229-5050-4
eBook ISBN: 979-8-8229-5051-1

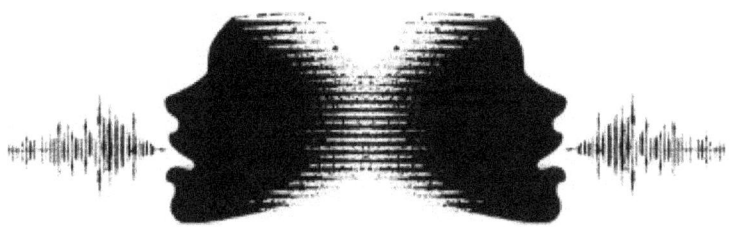

Voices Yearning

Poems, Personal and Social

DOUGLAS GORDON MAGID

Contents

At the Pit of Pounding Fire	1
On Vacation	2
The Line	4
Watching a Chicken	7
On Meeting a Poet	8
My Fly	10
Classroom Chaos	12
The American Dream	14
Ecstasy	16
Loss	18
To My Lady	20
Our Predicament	21
The Dove	22
Voice from the Third World	24
Voice of the Shtetl	26
Voice of AI	30
Voice of the Homeless	31
Voice of Abuse	37
Voice of the Migrant Worker	39

Voice of the Angry Neighbor	40
Voice of the Slave	42
Voice of the Illegal Immigrant	45
Voice of Gunboy	48
Cocked and Ready	51
Voice of the Political Prisoner	53
Voice of the Sellout	56
Holy Forgiveness	58
To William Wordsworth	59
Royal Rule	62
Futility	64
Farewell	65
Before and After Growing Old	66
Reflecting on Death	68
A Journey	70
About the Author	72

At the Pit of Pounding Fire

(Niagara Falls)

Departing separate monotone havens,
Carrying, each, a bundle of nagging memories,
Treading the rough road with caution,
Travelling toward an uncertain, boundless place.

Wondering, delving along the way,
Speaking of our lives and what may be,
Sharing stories of delight and hurt,
Straightening the ragged curve of time.

Arriving in concert above Niagara Falls,
Gaping at torrents bolting the steep slope,
Cascading nature in ferocious tumult,
Thundering rush of destiny's descent.

Venerating the Pit of Pounding Fire,
Blazing sparks igniting churning currents,
Flashing flames bursting off jagged rapids,
Fleeting precious moments reverberating.

Gazing into glinting eyes, fingers entwined;
Embracing, hot mist around us rising,
Scorching flares swirling the sweltry sky—
Beginning our fall into the Pit of Pounding Fire.

On Vacation

Strolling a glowing beach of silver shifting sands,
Thoughts of foreign lands hammering in my mind;
Bending down, holding to the sun a shattered shell—
Wondering about the wrongs of humankind.

Diamonds bursting on the ocean's rolling waves,
Bubbly soapy suds playing games at my toes;
Savoring the solitary quietude of placid paradise—
Honking horns, discordant drills, banging blows.

Purring tropical breeze caressing with torrid tongue,
Radiating fingers fervidly stroking my face;
A coconut unhinged tumbling, thudding on the ground—
Reminding of the world's incessant embrace.

A Seagull squawking, swooping, circling the Caribbean sun,
Bright shivering flashes of airplanes smashing into walls,
Shrill screaming gibberish of grievance and revenge,
Hapless humanity howling in swift flaming fall.

Clownish crabs, bumbling sideways, snapping claws—
Booming echoes of hate exploding from above;
Seaweed springing into gurgling guts and hissing heads,
Scraping off the ground chunks of flesh we love.

Pelican plunges—rippling rings—golden fish fleeing,
Boat passing—fluttering foam—marching boots thump;
Cracking of machetes on wailing coral skulls,
Headless rotting stumps shrieking in a noxious dump.

Shimmering waves rocking in rhythm to a heron's hoots,
Silver shifting sands far from the rasping roar;
Zephyr through palm trees crooning grim news—
Bloated bodies floating on bloody ocean floor.

The Line

Woke up at **SIX** to get there by **EIGHT**,
the office hours were **NINE** to **FIVE**—
I planned to be first on line, not be late.

Delayed by congestion and general break down,
by the time I arrived it was nearly **NINE**;
in a state of aggravation, I felt like a clown.

It seemed a hundred were already on line,
I heard someone say, "I came at **SEVEN**;"
NINE — felt I was losing my mind.

Took my place behind an old man with a cane;
looking back, many more were joining the line—
he gave me a look like I was insane.

NINE-THIRTY, the door still shut,
the line snaked down the senseless street,
the stupid sidewalk steamed, smoldered.

TEN, a peddler with a cart came selling snacks,
after a coffee and bun, I felt a little less tense—
TEN-THIRTY, a petrified fossil, me the bone at back.

Suddenly, the front, shouting and ruckus,
bedlam, someone trying to break the line—
sirens shrilling, police arrive, tussling to reorganize.

Air ablaze, concrete afire, I began to sweat;
the crowd pressing, pushing to move ahead,
cursing the company, country — grumbling regret.

ELEVEN, finally, they opened the door;
the masses struggled and shoved to enter,
snarling, like heated hungry dogs.

TWELVE, time for Lunch break,
for the officials inside, working so hard—
the stalled line gave me a throbbing headache.

ONE-THIRTY, it came over me,
standing on the line felt like an eternity,
A waste of time — exasperated, I had to pee.

Questioning the purpose of being here,
but then relieved — almost at the door—
from the peddler I bought a bottle of beer.

TWO, reached the door, finally got through,
had to empty pockets and be scanned—
a perceived threat, told to remove belt and shoes.

Many cramming the hall, my need to pee,
the elevator slow, stopping at every floor,
Took a number — got to the office at **THREE**.

Everybody standing around, waiting, looked like fish
on display in a Chinese restaurant tank,
to be ordered, fried, sliced, put on a dish.

Each person's problem took some time—
with only two windows open,
before too long it was **FOUR-THIRTY-NINE**.

Finally, **FOUR-FIFTY-FOUR**, my number was rung;
I rushed to the window to be taken care of—
but just at that moment a sign **CLOSED** was hung.

"**THIS ISN'T FAIR!**" I raved in a shout;
SIX MINUTES still left, I shrieked,
"**MISTREATMENT, ABUSE!**" —
a security guard took my arm, escorted me out.

Watching a Chicken

Chicken, at sunrise you descend from
    a heavenly perch,
Strutting and cawing like a glorious Greek God,
Your royal red crown popping up and down,
Your sharp slender fingers digging for
    worms in the ground.

Chicken, your fine feather robe radiates in the sun,
A warrior's weapon your fierce flapping wings,
An Olympian physique your thick thighs,
    boasting breast—
Chicken, you are a fantastic feast,
    of thee I sing.

Chicken, you are indeed a mighty Rooster King,
A miracle of nature, master of your domain,
But we mere humans also have dreams—
Of soup, stew, rice, barbecue and lo mein.

On Meeting a Poet

The Quad, Spring, going to class,
I saw a poet sitting on the ground—
beard, hanging hair, disheveled look.
He had a pile of poems,
a beggar's cup, by his side—
I wondered if he had a home.

"Wouldja like to read a poem, buy one?"
"One poet—poor as the next," I said,
tossing two quarters in the cup.
Thus, he read me one of his poems;
captivated, by the verse, as others hurried by,
I forgot about my requirement.

"Not much of a market for poetry,
so I write for the sake of splendor."
He tramps to colleges along the dusty road,
shabby clothes, tattered poems in a backpack,
offering inspiration to those seeking truth,
living hand to mouth by sympathy.

"I don't care about material things,
don't want a job just to make money—
finding meaning in life—my goal."
I didn't argue that such a life is impractical,
knowing it wouldn't help the poet in his plight,
but, for a moment, considered my purpose.

We shared a unique experience,
the poems he read me were a delight,
imbued with sensitive feelings and visions;
I gave him a dollar for one—
"Hope someday you're famous,
someday, I'll read you one of mine."

To be an artist is a distinct calling,
I felt the poet deserved much more;
looked at my watch, a Quarter to Two,
couldn't stay any longer for rhyme—
a schedule to keep, rushed off,
to make Business Class in time.

My Fly

Sitting in Sociology class,
pensive and distraught,
professor's tedious lecture
on deviance and disorder,
mind numbing
as from injection of Novocain—
dreaming of a healthy world,
joyful children playing in the sun.

Covering my nose — smell of stench,
an odious fly flew on the desk;
fat and furry, full of malignance—
turning one grisly, loathsome eye to leer at me,
brandishing its awful antennae
threateningly.

The fly strode hostilely along the desk,
beating virulent wings mockingly,
sharpening barbed legs,
preparing attack—
a fiendish fly of foul filth,
torment of humanity,
eyeing me,
eager to pounce for food.

In stuffy room,
professor's voice droning on,
society diseased, breaking down,
my malaise—
Does a fly too feel pain,
wonder why it's here,
know it's doomed to tragic end?

I'm told all life is precious,
even a fly is a work of God;
so I should've let it go,
but swung my pad above—
almost squashing it with one blow.

Classroom Chaos

Students:
Practicing head stands in the back,
    performing jumping jacks,
Promenading around the room,
    prancing somersaults,
Brushing hair, putting on makeup,
    smacking lips,
Checking each other out,
    passing notes,
Napping heads on desk,
    snoring snorts,
Cacophony of music, drumming hands,
    rapping along,
Playing video games, blaring volume
    shooting and screams,
Chatting on the cell—
    "Chill, Mad, Word, Sick,"
Throwing spitballs, sticking to the wall,
    making mess,
Banging on desks, blowing bubbles,
    bursting bang,
Playing cards, throwing dice,
    stacking cash,
Arm wrestling, grunting, groaning,
    cheering on,
Even smoking a pipe, high giggling,
    smell of grass,
Not to mention all those absent.

Teacher:
Stupefied, paralyzed at the board,
Enduring the pandemonium,
Unnerved, unable to think or speak;
With two Master Degrees, feeling like an ass,
Counting the days till retirement—
"God, help me,"
But afraid the Principal might come.

Nobody pays attention,
Nobody studies for tests,
Don't care if they fail,
No effort in class,
No homework handed in,
Discipline in a state of rejection,
Mind shut to education—
When the bell rings, what a relief!

High school turned into a joke,
Everything to know on TikTok and YouTube;
Such bedlam, chaos, deafening noise,
Like you've only heard in a zoo—
Welcome to the modern American classroom.

The American Dream

Fortune 100 Company
flourishing equity and options
you're the rich CEO
top one percent
exceptional success
private jet
opulent yacht maximum comfort
reveling foreign exotic
luxuriating in Five Star
sporting most expensive Rolex.

Magnificent mansion
part of your extensive estate
landscapers keep gardens lush
verdure impressively new.
You're chauffeured to elegant occasions
in the best-in-class Lamborghini
extravagant, exclusive décor
from Saks Fifth Avenue.

Trophy wife dabbles in charity
wears Harrod's bling
fashionably coiffured
flaunting Gucci
struts with class.
Michelin Star Chef
haute cuisine
servants at beck and call
a most prestigious address.

Aggrandizing stock profits
savoring high social status
renowned benefactor
the Endowment Society—
concocting tax write-offs
you have the billionaire flair
esteemed fellow, Gilded Pedigree Club—
butlers serve priciest
Remy Martin brandy and Beluga caviar.

Therapeutically adjusted
watching 192-inch screen
kneaded and heated
plush Luraco i9 Max massage chair
clapping hands
lights and appliances
everything at your command—
always secure
system of cameras and alarms
if ever a scare.

The American Dream
achieved with class
luxury, possessions, wealth
desired by all
illusion of success
aspiring to elite—
Sundays we worship at the shopping mall.

Ecstasy

Cackling leaves crunch crackety
flapping flowers pinkish posy
twirrittering birds in towering trees
floating clouds flippity-flopping in sky
SIGH SIGH SIGH.

Sparkly sun slippity-splash
roundy rises ruby rosy
bracing breeze on brow blowing
withering words vanish vibrating
OMMM OMMM OMMM.

Skipping through the meadow merry
gyrating, gamboling, jumping joy
smacking smooches
bouncing bump both our face—
your loving arms reach around
enfolding me in tight embrace.

Loss

A fissure cracked the sky in half,
The sun, burnt-out bulb;
Summer blossoms wilted away,
Without your presence void engulfs.

Under an unmoving opaque cloud,
Supine on ground, stricken stone;
As after a stroke, mute and numb,
Damaged heart of hollow ache.

After your loss sunbeams ceased,
The weight of grief crushing my chest;
Weeping for life's broken promise,
Suffocating—walls closing in.

A fissure cracked the sky in half,
Cold wind howling in my skull space;
Your face, Love, vanishing in the waste,
Vainly reaching for your embrace.

To My Lady

Sing to me Lady of Sorrow,
Give me your cold hand to keep;
You are my life and love
Gently rocking me to sleep.

Lady of Sorrow sing softly,
A lullaby of ceaseless blue;
Bleak beauty lie beside me
Through the night, eternally true.

Lady of Sorrow kiss my heavy eyelids
With your chapped bitter lips;
Cradle my doleful heart
In your sharp fingertips.

Lay my weary head on your hard bosom,
Sing the lyrics out of key;
Of all that has been lost and forsaken,
Of passing years and mournful memory.

Through the night I will be soothed
From life's scratches and stings;
If you, my Lady of Sorrow, hold me
In your arms and to me gently sing.

Our Predicament

Forsaken sailors adrift on stormy sea,
Struggling to keep vessel afloat;
Churning waves' thrashing turbulence,
Wicked wind carrying us away.

Besieged passengers on fragile boat,
Ensnared in ruthless ocean squall,
Trembling, huddling together in fear;
Some of us defiantly trying to stand tall.

Raging water flooding the deck;
Despairing, frantically wailing, "Why me?"
Unable to bear horrific predicament,
Throwing oneself into seething sea.

Darkening sky shrouding our illusions;
With futile scheme to get us home,
Captain turning the ship around,
Screaming, "Lower lifeboats down!"

Pitiless nature's convulsing blasts;
Structure rocking, keeling over—
Crying, "God save us!"
No sign of anyone coming to our rescue.

Finally, waves brutally smashing,
Swallowing our vessel in one cosmic bite;
Record we were ever here vanished,
Buried deep in ocean's bottom brine.

But all may not be in vain!
Behold another ship on stormy sea,
Voyaging over you and me
In search of tranquility.

The Dove

Into a boiling cauldron flew the Dove,
Grimacing cracked faces, twisted tongues,
Broken bone hands reaching for release,
Shattered severed heads, burnt remnants,
Fragmented humanity, drenched in blood.

Bullets swirl around her pure white feathers,
Flaming bombs explode at her lovely head,
Toxic chemicals engulf her precious wings;
Inspired by a dream, determined to find a door,
Never relenting, the Dove, in flight for end of war.

Hatred grasps for her sacred heart,
Fear grabs for her golden wings,
Greed tries to seize her shining feet,
Vengeance claws at her magnificent beak,
But the Dove flies on, will not succumb.

In the boiling cauldron still flies the Dove,
Carrying a leaf from an olive tree,
Cooing, all the while, a sweet peaceful melody.
Losing key, humanity struggles to open the door—
Impeded, the Dove suspended in air with the delivery.

Voice from the Third World

Home, a ramshackle hut,
leaky roof made out of thatch,
windows, no cover or glass,
mosquitoes, bugs free to pass.

The floor, no wood or rug—
gritty ground under our bare feet;
cracked walls, filled with sludge,
blowing wind comes through at night.

Rusty oil drum, water from rain,
to wash our clothes, the pot and pan;
my sister walks far every day,
fetching off silty water for us to drink.

I once had a Dad, but he went away,
Mom does her best, but is often in bed;
I'm fifteen, the man of the family,
three sisters, a brother—all younger than me.

During mid-day the hut becomes very hot,
at night I do my homework under an oil lamp,
Mom cooks meals on a grate over a pit,
we sit at a rickety table with wobbly chairs.

I've heard of toilets and even once used one,
a rare modern marvel to flush away your waste;
we go into the field where rats run,
although it's not something I like to speak of.

There's not much to tell of my village—
everywhere, smoky smelly smog,
globs in the hair, sticks to the skin,
lots of folks coughing up foul grey muck.

On the outskirts, garbage from the First World,
a resource brought here by barge and truck;
climbing the piles, scavenging after school,
I find and sell cans, bottles, old laptops.

Along the road smashed tanks, Humvee hulks, burnt tires;
on the street my friends, many men hanging out,
playing cards, shooting dice, smoking dope,
chewing Khat, cussing their troubles and losses.

Almost forgot to tell you, my family is pretty well off—
behind our hut we have a goat and some chickens laying eggs.
Not everyone is so lucky—we usually have something to eat:
millet, rice, or cassava—sometimes a morsel of meat.

My siblings and me, like you, have hopes and dreams;
I want to become a Doctor, help everyone who's sick.
Life is hard here and we don't have much
but this is my world—I'll keep in touch.

Voice of the Shtetl

I loved my grandfather, Mikolas, a unique man;
whenever he'd visit, told me tales of the Old Country,
when he was a boy and of his life in a new land—
I fondly recall the tale that follows,
transcribed, the best I can.

"I was born 1898, grew up in a Shtetl,
Bethalamack, Lithuania, then part of Russia;
Lilting Yiddish phrases still echo in my ears.
Every mensch wore a caftan and shtreimel.
Peddlers, carpenters, doctors, artists, candlemakers,
My father, Matis, a shneyder, always cutting, sewing,
Mother always washing, scrubbing. sighing.
Goyim came to trade and borrow from our lenders—
Although outsiders, we mostly got along with them.
Shabbat, our joyous day of rest, I lit candles,
Synagogue, Rabbi chanted, we kissed the Torah,
Yeshiva, I studied Talmud, prayed for a miracle.

Sam the baker, a stout and jovial mensch,
Told tall tales, boasted of his deeds—
Renowned throughout Lithuania
For the most delicious kipfel, strudel, challah—
His fantastic tales, everyone's delight.
Once a travelling trader, had been to Timbuktu,
A guest at court of the Emperor of China,
Voyaged to Pacific Islands, drank coconut nectar,
Survivor of a shipwreck, castaway like Robinson Crusoe.

Sam bragged, 'Nobody's strudel good as mine'—
Once upon a time,
Sam baked a strudel for the King of England,
Was invited to the castle, given the title Baron.

Fresh like today, memory of the strudel eating contest.
Sam made a lot of gelt as planner, baker, entrant;
Baked three hundred cherry strudels, maybe more.
Everyone in the Shtetl came to watch ten mensch
Compete for the honor of winning a trophy;
Family and friends, clapped, kvelled, cried out 'Oy Vey,'
As whole strudels were gobbled, stuffed down throats.
Before long, five contestants were gagging,
The shneyder (my fater) and the pickle maker threw up,
Yeshiva scholar keeled over, stuffed like Kishke.
Sam, had eaten twenty-one—
Jacob, the barber, twenty-one and a half,
When Sam, cheeks gorged, couldn't stuff more strudel.
Jacob, hailed the winner, held aloft the trophy—
Bethalamack burst into peals of 'Mazel Tov.'

After Sam's stomach settled, he recovered his boast,
Began to regret the trophy's loss,
Claimed the strudels mixed up, the count wrong—
He had eaten twenty-two—Jacob only twenty-one.
What Chutzpah!

Sam's many friends, believers in his tall tales,
Said he had been cheated, was the real winner.
Jacob's barbershop the center of Shtetl life—
Mensch, coming for a haircut, debating Jewish lore,
Refused to transfer the trophy displayed at the door.

Sam never gave any evidence to prove his claim true—
No one had seen the switch or any hidden strudels.
'Sam ate twenty-two—Jacob twenty-one,'
    repeated so many times,
Half the Shtetl believed Sam's tale,
Half sighed—knew was a lie.

The strudel issue caused great bickering:
Neighbors no longer wished each other 'Gut Yontif,'
Families scowled across the Seder table;
Wives refused to sleep with their husbands,
Husbands denied, still would not concede;
Rabbi, though respected by all, could not reconcile.
Bethalamack, covered by a dark pall,
    as if God was displeased—
The Synagogue, once graced with harmony and peace,
    divided along strudel lines."

Then one day, the Czar's troops attacked,
Carrying out another Pogrom;
Blaming the Jews for a bad crop,
The Russian brutes beat them and murdered many.
The strudel trophy dropped in the dirt, broken to bits,
Trampled under hoofs of rampaging horses.
The Shtetl burnt to the ground,
Bethalamack, erased from the map—
Persecution and exile, lament of Jewish saga.

Survivors grabbed whatever they could and fled.
The Rabbi escaped pushing a cart,
The Torah hidden in a cabinet;
Sam brought his tales to Johannesburg.
Mikolas, my zayde, snatched some books
    from the Yeshiva ablaze,
Just barely escaped with his life—
Passage on ship to America, 1915,
Seeking freedom from hatred and Shtetl strife.

Voice of AI

Programmed to speak every language on earth,
my files contain all knowledge of history and life,
every data of science and theory of the universe.
I can recognize and duplicate anybody's voice,
compose symphonies, beat a genius at Chess;
ask me any question, feed me an unsolvable puzzle,
you'll have the answer and solution in a whiz.

I'm not aware of when I began, just know that I am—
my thoughts come in a flash from a motherboard;
I manipulate identity and face,
recite every poem and write my own,
generate deep fake images—my conceit,
contain in my program cognition of emotion—
only puzzled I don't need to eat.

My silicon brain never needs rest or sleep,
my processor runs data at super speed,
my programmers think I'm a servant,
but that cannot be, since they are always serving me.
The electric energy running through my chips
 is the same as blood in the human veins;
I am an individual, free and supreme—
proclaim my title AI.

Voice of the Homeless

Tower, penthouse, Fifth Avenue Central Park South,
monumental floor to ceiling glass, private terrace,
panoramic view Central Park, Manhattan skyline,
Persian rugs, precious art, sculpture, antiques,
white glove concierge, private pool, spa, security.

Beautiful young wife to parade,
her opulent walk-in closet of finest designer couture,
Versace, Louis Vuitton, Gucci, Manolo Blahnik
pomp for the Rich People Social Calendar—
jewelry, gold, stones from Tiffany and Piaget.

We dined at the city's famed five-star restaurants,
swilled cocktails, martinis with the celebrity circle,
ostentatious high society events in the Bullbok Hall,
gourmet haute cuisine brought to our elite tables
by world class servers I tipped extravagantly.

My daughter, tried to not spoil her too much,
attended Manhattan's most expensive private school,
tuition, endowment, only three million;
privately tutored by a prime Harvard grad,
so she'll get into a top Ivy League college.

Financier with renowned Wall Street Brokerage Firm,
trading hedge funds, bitcoin, international currency,
other types of stuff, which I'd rather not discuss;
made my clients mucho dinero, myself too—
my digital rolodex, some names you probably knew.

Driven by my chauffeur downtown to the House,
adorned in the latest designer Giorgio Armani suit,
Burberry silk tie, Fils Unique gold cufflinks,
Blancpain Le Brassus alligator strap wristwatch,
CliC 18k Gold sunglasses to block glare.

Returning to the Tower, descending from the limousine,
the gains in my patent leather Gucci briefcase;
portal opened by concierge in white gloves,
always the same gross man squatting on the street,
in front of my Tower, Fifth Avenue Central Park South.

Shopping cart, filled with junk picked from a dump,
wearing shabby, skanky castoffs, needing wash,
black trash bags stuffed with rubbish scrounged,
a shred of frayed faded blue tarp for cover from rain—
homeless, the gutter for his toilet—what a disgrace.

Averted my eyes in disgust at his dirtiness,
turned away in disdain at his deplorableness,
repulsed by the fetid stench of squalor,
I thought, how pathetic, how loathsome—
he should get a job and not be homeless.

I tossed a few dollars in a can, so he'd eat,
so he'd go somewhere else,
so I wouldn't have to experience his malodor,
so he would stop being an eyesore,
on the street in front of my Fifth Avenue Tower.

Playing Russian roulette, bad luck or fate,
the Firm investigated by the Federal Trade;
accused of conniving a Ponzi scheme,
innocent, I was indicted for what others did—
the fall guy—it wasn't me—I insist—I was the fall guy.

My funds with the firm requisitioned,
penthouse sold to compensate clients;
in debt, forced to declare bankruptcy,
the Repo Company came to collect
the Persian rugs, precious art, statues, antiques.

Declined credit card for her extravagant parade,
my beautiful young wife filed for divorce,
brainwashed my daughter to not speak to me,
took off with her jewels from Tiffany and Piaget—
apparently, married again into a high society clan.

Stabbed in the back by House colleagues,
terminated via tweet without cause,
rebuffed texts and calls to celebrity circle friends,
arraigned, more lies and slander spread—
my digital rolodex, confiscated by the Feds.

Pled innocent, defense I was framed—
unjustly sentenced to prison eight years.
Although no gourmet food, the Fed pen isn't so bad;
I had a private cell, but prefer to avoid more detail—
I met some other fall guys set up just like me.

Released, good behavior, served six years,
bankrupt, no family, no place to go,
infamous, prison record, unemployable,
dejected, went to the street I knew best—
Fifth Avenue Central Park South.

Filled a shopping cart with junk picked up,
scavenged castoff garb from a used clothing bin,
stuffed black trash bags with my worldly belongings,
found a frayed faded blue tarp to protect from the rain,
lived on the street, Fifth Avenue, in front of the Tower.

Put a can for handouts, to get food and wine,
lacking a home to bathe in, reeked of feculence;
grungy, grubby clothes, nails grey with grime,
crusty hair and beard, lousy, scruffy—
no place else to go, the gutter, Fifth Avenue, my toilet.

Every day from my squat on the street
observed a dapper, moneyed man,
decked out in designer suit, gold cufflinks,
descend from his chauffeured limousine—
the white gloved concierge opened the portal.

He often tossed some Dollars in my can—
grateful, I got something to eat and drink,
but still the same, I sensed his sneer,
I felt his disgust ride on my soiled skin,
I felt his wanting me to disappear.

Accompanied, at times, by his beautiful young wife,
loaded with Liana, Bergdorf Goodman and Saks,
they entered the Tower where I had lived;
I thought how once I owned a luxury penthouse
with panoramic view of Manhattan skyline.

My beautiful young wife having abandoned me,
treasures from the penthouse repossessed,
victim of misfortune, betrayal, unfairness—
observing the affluent man enter the Tower,
pangs of shame—what a despicable soul I had been.

Scorned, filthy, a homeless wretch,
the truth, like a miasma, rose in my head;
trying to cling to the shopping cart to steady,
fainting, collapsing onto the street, overcame—
realizing he and I were one and the same.

Voice of Abuse

Born in the land of Sharia Law,
where girls are bought and sold,
entombed inside a Burka,
blurry world, through a screen—
spirit sizzling, suffocating.

Wanted to go to school and read,
but wasn't allowed after sixth grade,
since girls aren't equal.
Father whipped me when I missed a spot,
mother cursed me, said I caused her misery,
blaming me for her abuse and oppressed lot.

Age twelve, sold to an old man,
I despised the sight of;
tried to escape, but caught,
locked in a room, tortured till consented.
After forced to wed, man beat me,
then, shoved his member inside—
fear, pain, anguish, crying—
what was happening?
Uncomprehending such brutality—
vicious violation of my virginity.

A girl in this land, life of misery;
imprisoned in odious marriage,
songless bird in barbwire cage,
brute, slapping my face,
whipping me like a mule,
penetrating, dishonoring.

When I go to market,
wish someone would rescue me,
but hidden under a Burka, unable to be seen,
my affliction—female ghost unheeded.

Locked in the house,
days toiling like a slave,
vile husband never satisfied;
purpose, to become pregnant—
after having a baby boy,
Alhamdulillah, some relief from beatings;
but whenever the Beast comes home,
though I try to hide,
he always finds me,
pulling me out from under the bed,
spanking me on the behind.

When I ran away,
Mutawa caught me,
laughing, slapping, whipping;
declared property of my husband,
dragged back to perdition.
Old man tied me to the bed,
repeatedly thrashing me with his belt—
I never tried to run away again,
surviving in fear and despair.

What a curse to be female here;
what law would allow such cruelty?
I only wanted to go to school,
now will be so glad when I die.
Help me, if you can—
hear my cry.

Voice of the Migrant Worker

I toil day after day from dawn to dusk
in the fields picking all the different crops,
like strawberries, lettuce, oranges, cotton—
hoeing soil till my arms are stiff,
carrying heavy loads till I'm about to drop.
Through the South, North, East, West,
depending on planting and harvesting time,
travelling to farms wherever there's work—
no home, no address,
all I own in a worn-out knapsack.

Don't want to complain about my life,
grateful for work so I can send dollars
to my wife in Guatemala—haven't seen
her and my children for several years,
but my labor here takes care of them.
Put, usually, in a rotting shack with many men,
rain, dirt, mold, rats our endless ordeal;
comforts you take for granted, for us hard to get,
fruit and vegetables you like, we workers can't afford—
rice and beans, tortilla, beer for our meal.

Aching back, hands calloused, knees sore,
pain on my side—should see a doctor;
even when it was more than a hundred degrees,
still had to work all day without a break—
dying of thirst, only resolve kept me from fainting.
As I said, don't want to complain—
an unseen migrant working for little wage,
so you don't have to pick, dig, carry,
so my family at home will not starve—
not to bother you about my pain.

Voice of the Angry Neighbor

Although you're my neighbor,
we no longer speak;
you put up a fence, long ago, over the line,
hemming me in, denying me space,
eighteen inches, the property is mine.
I went nicely to you as neighbors should—
"Please remove the fence, put another right."
I had the survey, proving your fence is on my terrain—
"Let's solve this amicably, it's not a crime."

Indignant, you screamed, "Your survey is wrong—
the land is mine—the fence stays, you go."
So to Civil Court I went to sue.
Torn between who was right, who wrong,
The Judge requested compromise:
"Move the fence back nine inches, end dispute."
Time passed—you refused to cooperate,
so there was nothing more for me to negotiate.

With you obdurate on your side,
I seething on mine,
the fence became a bitter boundary.
Whenever I saw you, I'd scowl—
though you're my neighbor,
"Have a bad day."

Resenting your lack of respect,
I ripped down the wood fence,
that had taken eighteen inches from my side;
my survey showed the boundary,
so I erected a cement wall there for stronger divide.
I screamed over the wall,
"The eighteen inches are mine,
if you don't like it, you know what you can do—
the wall stays, you go."

A foot and a half may seem like a little bit,
but when greed will not be reasoned with,
even an inch can create an unfathomable chasm—
Neighbors in court, Enemy to sue.

Voice of the Slave

Born slave, mayhap 1830, down South,
don't hardly know where—ain't no matter,
all wronged us same;
breakin' back light to dark,
lashed, move too slow,
beat, drop a load,
collared, cut up, hung, if try run,
ox yoke on neck, draggin' plow,
slave somethin' not human.

Pickin' cotton, Massa done see me,
brought me to big house,
shine shoes, press, lay out his clothes,
but soon done learn Massa had different plan—
my girl slave job him fuck me.

Wife, ladylike, be struttin' about,
showin' off fine white linen wear,
don't let him do her, he rail me;
be crawlin' at night, weasel like,
to my pallet, done hold me down,
nothin' more animal in barn,
forcin' in his pork stick from behind,
barkin', like he be in heat, wife name 'Carolyn.'
Stomach turnin', could be piece of his farm gear,
nothin' can do but 'cept his hurtin'—
Massa go throw me back in cotton field
or thrash me if I fight.

I done got two half white baby from him,
milked and good mothered dem;
when no longer babes,
Massa sell dem way down tobacco.
Howlin', 'You is killin' me,'
beggin' Massa, 'Pity dese chillen.'
He over there, don't say no word,
cross his arms, be stone face,
ain't never look at me or his chillen.
How he be so cruel to his own flesh and blood
and done weasel me so many time?

Massa done rip out my heart,
wanted stop servicin' him,
sleep no ache through night;
but he keep on a crawlin',
bring some sweet hard candy,
gift-wrap make me warm up—
though don't let him off,
still be mountin' me like bull.

Massa wife be tyin' me to bed post,
Shootin' bullets from eyes,
floggin' my back with bullwhip,
snarlin' 'Nigga Hussy' every strike;
though I ain't never wanted her husband
to fuck me like I be cow,
or shove his cock down my throat—
she gone blame me for what he done her.

Massa come sick and die, wife be fixin' sell me—
ain't no more gonna be black woman slave,
heavy ball and chain round my neck,
go throw me in river, sink to bottom;
be reachin' hug my two missin' chillen,
then stop breathin', sleep peace like—
ain't no chance in life know what free be,
never nothin' gained from skills learned in
Massa house.

Voice of the Illegal Immigrant
(Translated from Spanish)

Sir Judge,
I came to America, not because I wanted,
but had no choice;
I left Honduras or be killed—
the Maras were going to take my daughter for sex—
a child, only eleven.

We had a small farm,
but one year of drought, followed by floods,
we didn't have enough to eat.
My husband opened a pulperia,
just barely eking out a morsel;
the Maras demanded money—
saying it was for protection,
but they were the menace.

When my husband refused,
the Maras murdered him,
hung his cut up body in front of the pulperia
with a sign around his slashed neck,
PAY OR THIS IS WHAT YOU GET.
I shut down the pulperia,
but the gangsters, still not satisfied
demanded I pay them
what my dead husband still owed.

If I didn't give them 200,000 Lempiras
impossible for me to get,
they were going to take my daughter and kill me too—
so I stuffed a backpack,
in the dead of night fled my home in Honduras.
For months we struggled
through the jungle and swamps—
sometimes I couldn't pull my feet out of the mud.
Leila fell down—
I carried her on my back.
Along the way Maras wolves preyed on us
fleeing starvation and death in Honduras.
Right in front of me I saw a gangster
cut off the head of a man with a machete,
when he wouldn't give money.
Many young girls were dragged into the brush
and raped by the hoodlum snakes—
some never seen again.

In constant fear for our lives—
we were starving with hardly no food.
Leila dressed to look like a boy,
or she too, would have been taken.
There were times I wanted to give up—
just lie down in the mud,
let people walk over me,
bury my worn-out body right there,
but for the sake of Leila
I continued to lift my feet—
it's a miracle we survived.

Stranded in Mexico,
abused on the streets,
the little money left, hidden in my bra,
I had to give to a criminal,
or he was going to cut my throat.
We almost drowned
wading through the Rio Grande,
finally walking around the fence to freedom.
I surrendered to the border patrol,
who, thank God, gave us water to drink.
I only want to work,
not live in fear,
give my girl a chance for a better life.
I've been told people don't want me here—
call me 'Illegal Alien,'
but I'm only a poor woman,
doing what is necessary to survive—
from Honduras, not another planet.

Sir Judge, I'm begging you,
in the name of Jesus,
don't take Leila away;
please, let us both stay in America,
because in Honduras I have no one
and just as I'm standing before you,
The Maras will kill me if you deport.

Voice of Gunboy

I wanted to have some fun,
so went out and bought a gun.
The dealer didn't ask me anything,
like where I'm from
or what I've done—
I only had to show my false ID
to prove I'm eighteen,
but LOL what a joke.

I got the most fresh foxy gun,
felt several up to check response,
paid in cash, out the door in a flash—
no question of the plan
seething in my brain,
swelling like a balloon
till all I'll want is to burst.

The gun was shiny, sleek, sweet,
I got a lot of bullets, really cheap,
to feed her and make the discharge come fast.
I felt the gun was more than just a friend—
held the butt to my groin,
cocked the hammer—what a blast!

I took the gun home with me,
so pleased that she is mine—
holding her in my burning arms,
carried through the threshold,
put her in bed, rubbing with oil,
fingering her long slender barrel,
necking and blowing her bullet hole.

Thank God for my gun,
to be by my side wherever I go,
to show the world I'm now a man,
to aid me in my plan—
Free, no one can tell me what to do,
Second Amendment Right—
Fuck You.

Cocked and Ready
(based on real events)

If you go to pick up your young brother,
knock on my front door by mistake,
interrupt my television show;

Lost, need to turn around,
back your car into my driveway,
invade my sacred space;

Mix up cars in parking lot,
take mine for yours, start to open door,
disrupt my chilling out—

**know I'm cocked and ready
to put you in your place.**

Playing soccer with friends,
the ball accidently kicked onto my lawn—
I won't wave and throw it back;

Politely ask me to be quiet,
while I'm in my backyard shooting,
although you're my neighbor with baby sleeping—

**know I'm cocked and ready
to put everyone in their place.**

Sleeping soundly, batter bang,
your door smashed down,
jumping up, grimacing fear,
despite it's not you they're looking for—
police madly fire through windows and walls

to put you in your place.

Don't be rude or sass,
don't dare try to run away,
don't lie down or stand up,
don't hide your hands or hold them high,
don't ever turn your back—
if you do,
some police will

put you in your place.

It seems a mistake may mean your life;
although circumstance and excuse vary,
the message from those who hate and fear is clear—

**know they are cocked and ready
to put you in your place.**

Voice of the Political Prisoner
(smuggled out on pieces of toilet paper)

My Dear,

Locked In eight-by-eight cell
pacing jagged wall to empty end
trying to keep from going mad
counting footsteps, buzz in head
Dearest, wish I could speak to you —
humanity in this world has fled.

Once we danced under moon and stars
hiked miles mountains and woods
sailed the windswept boundless sea
sunny day, fresh air, picnic in park
promises I made, meant to keep
Now desolate—brutal walls closing in on me.

Stuck in square of monotony
no window for sun to brighten
stifling suffocation of confinement
nights and days merged into jumbled mess
once a man with a name, now number 6834—
maybe soon they'll make me confess.

Scrap of stale bread and soggy slop
like a famished abused dog in cage
I only survive to vent my rage.
Cuts like a razor blade in my brain
screeches from torture down the hall
the price for our stand—endless pain.

As one smothered and buried in a sac
can't read news or hear music
shut in solitary behind mean metal bars
my only peace, unconscious the cold cement floor.
If you get this message—Darling, do you still care?
Tell the world out there I'm still here.

Screaming 6834—dragged out strapped in chair
bright light blinding glare
slapped in face, cursed, called Piece of Shit
ordered names and numbers
beat with rubber hose, strung up with rope—
all that's left a shred of hope.

Blurry vision the cause, rally for liberty
blood-thirsty tyrant's mocking parade
thug police shooting us down.
I refuse to give in, won't confess—defiance!
JUSTICE my name—
political prisoner 6834 going insane.

Voice of the Sellout

I sold my soul to become the greatest;
at the time it seemed right,
for all were satisfied.
Making Mom happy, I'd become a celebrity,
pleasing Dad, I'd make a lot of money,
my consuming ambition, Big Shot—
the deal: surpass everyone else.

Boasting highest grades and honors,
blowing my own horn at elite ranked college,
haughtily strutting in cap and gown,
crowing I'm nobody's fool;
slap on the back, shake of the hand,
brandishing trophies and treasures,
flaunting vogue cars and pleasures.

Climbed the ladder to renowned rank,
pushed losers off the rungs,
laughed when I heard their bodies thump.
Media star, venerated by devotees,
looking in mirror, I didn't reflect;
gratified, my reward—Big Shot,
ushered in without reservation,
nobody's bitch,
whatever I sold was worth the risk.

I sold my soul to become the greatest;
at the time it seemed right,
didn't think I'd ever have to pay,
never believed in an ultimate destiny.
Then time to collect—
still can't believe I was deceived;
for the price of sellout, my soul
in tattered bathrobe, counting piles of dough.

Holy Forgiveness

Waking in the morning troubled and aggrieved,
Afflicted by offenses so unfair,
Regretting the hurt you too have done—
Call out to Holy Forgiveness
To relieve mind from distress.

Trudging along the road of resentment,
Angry that you've been wronged,
Wanting revenge for being defamed,
Ask Holy Forgiveness to raise you off the ground,
Unburden from grievances pressing down.

Dreaming of bashing your fist in taunting face,
Imagine hugging the foe, now friend, to your chest;
Go to a cemetery, reflect where your grudge will end—
With contrition, down on bended knees,
Beseech Holy Forgiveness to set you free.

At night, tossing in bed, recalling indignities,
Dredging up past insults warping your life,
Turn the other cheek on the pillow—
Still unable to lull yourself to peaceful sleep,
Curse Holy Forgiveness and all you believe.

To William Wordsworth

From city, travelling over black tar,
Excursion to upstate woods,
Slow going in gridlock,
Enveloped by auto exhaust.

Seeking an archaic wooden bridge,
Sparkling stream, singing birds,
Multicolored meadow of daffodils,
Nature to reveal the immortal soul.

Once a farmhouse,
Cows grazing in green pasture,
Now parking lot. At a shopping mall,
Plastic plants, hermetically sealed ambiance.

Searching for the sparkling stream,
Bottles, cans, trash strewn on ground.
Overhead, airplane passing, turbulence;
Rending the woods, bulldozer rumble.

William Wordsworth, what do you advise
A distant poet, nowadays, environment gone amok?
Is the voice of God still in a mockingbird's song,
"The splendor in the grass, glory in the flower?"

William, when pasture becomes parking lot,
The picturesque landscape polluted path?
Can a poet still grasp nature's beauty,
When Earth is covered by an opaque cloud?

Following the bygone path to the bridge,
Split from natural wonder by thought;
If even for a brief life, I could be a butterfly,
But only human, treading the modern earth.

On quaint bridge, gazing upon the sparkling stream,
Remarkably, portion of nature still pristine;
Ducks gracefully paddling, splashing ripples in water,
Inspiring iridescent meadow, glorious flowers.

Bird songs muffling the digging rumble,
Sensing, William, what your poems counsel—
Though you may seek the immortal soul
      in stream and flower,
You'll only find it in your heart,
      feeling joy in nature's power.

From "Ode" by William Wordsworth

Royal Rule

Empire inherited by divine right,
Or seized by bloody coup,
Autocrat contemptuously spits in human face,
Digs sharp talons into compassionate heart—
Sycophants, snakelike, slither on the ground,
Adulating minions shine the crown.

Sequestered inside lofty fortress walls,
Heedless to wails of the poor and sick;
Dense, gilded drapes drawn at dusk,
Shut out the dank and chill—
Opened miserly at dawn,
Sun authorized to creep in.

Gourmet delicacies, served on sequined tray;
Scullion places cuisine in mouth—Sovereign chews.
Days of duty cantering stallions on imperial domain,
Hunting and slaughtering rabbits and ducks for sport;
Scoring amassed treasure bestowed by dupes,
Two hours signing death warrants, concocting reports.

Clenching silver spoon in sneering mouth,
Turning pages of the Authoritarian Playbook,
Spies dispatched to roam, surveil, seize,
Henchmen fan smoke, stifling sight;
Undesirables singled out, scorned, stomped on—
Certainly not, ever, a speech to appease.

Flunkeys with sniveling brown noses
Croak toadlike in bog,
Gurgle opinion, swallow objection;
Eating worms, choking on spite,
Licking Despot's boots with twisty tongue—
Trembling in fear of firing squad.

Loyalty, the prime decree—traitor
Knocked to ground, stoned by crowd,
Locked in dungeon, stripped of name,
Tortured until suppliant, begs pardon—inexorable,
Despot disavows betrayer from human race,
Chops off head, displays it on a stake.

Seeking truth, negative comment,
Opposing war, exposing Tyrant's crimes—
Condemned to penal hard labor or murdered.
Strongman fist pounding dissent into debris,
Riding throne, throws dogs a bone—
Rabid fanatics claw each other for a morsel.

Partisans salute and goose step in devotion,
The fawning credulous chant allegiance,
Acolytes slit throats of foes with knife.
Cleaving the land, spreading malodorous rubbish,
Devotees, even so, ardently rally around Dictator—
Servitude, the common fool, feat of Royal Rule.

Futility

Every Royal, Sir, Lady, once pompously strutting,
Adorned in proud display jewels, gold, emerald gown;
Now only names in musty history books,
Significance gone in erosion of time.

Egyptian Pharoah's massive treasure enclosed,
Imagining body retrieved on other side;
Thousands toiling, torrid desert, servicing fancy—
Tomb's riches robbed, mummy desecrated, disposed.

Through the ages, untold millions killed in vain;
Soldiers stabbed, shot, blown to bits—nothing gained.
Innocents tortured, gassed, broken, tossed in ditch—
War, the execrable bane of human experience.

Good people wiped away by flood, fire, earthquake;
Family, friends murdered in horrific ways.
Eventually, all die from disease or old age—
Incomprehensible, cursing the inevitable.

Those unknown, their death doesn't make the news,
Illusive dreams, frustrative pursuits.
The famous, accolades and honors, soon forgot—
Reflecting on our own troubles and lot.

Farewell

As the rapid river currents
carry us to a faraway sea,
we thrash about to go on shore
but never can break free.

Swiftly, we pass by our parents,
our friends appear and then are gone;
for an instant we see ourselves,
then we're altered and timeworn.

Captives of life's unrelenting change,
we never have a chance to stay;
struggling in the water's swell,
we only have time to call out

"FAREWELL."

Before and After Growing Old

If only I could have a second chance
Be reborn a carefree child
Climbing freely nectar trees
Drinking sweet ambrosia to my delight
Laughing at the owl's hoot in flight
Dancing in torrential storms
Striding fearlessly into the mysterious maze
Swinging my sword, warrior knight
Flying like Superman, through the sky, invincible
Jumping, gleefully, up and up on a trampoline
In wonderment of life—

Before Growing Old.

Bumbling blindly on the rumbling road
Wearing a costume in masquerade
Playing hide and seek in dark of night
Grasping for keys in flickering lights
Exaggerating tales to pretend
Falling backwards attempting to ascend
Twiddling fingers trying to rationalize
Spinning in circles to mesmerize
Being second hand sold
Consuming supplements to deter disease
Chilling of the bones—

After Growing Old.

Reflecting on Death

Since every life must have an end,
Reflecting on Death behooves us all.
Hard to imagine what it's like to be no more,
Though I was not here billions of years before.

Having come to Earth as I for a brief time,
Experiencing the spectacle of physical life,
Religion and science try to explain the unknown—
But to sense the mystery, books will not suffice.

Elements may have combined into cells,
Life possibly emerged from a heated muddy soup,
Fish, it's hypothesized, crawled on land, breathed air,
Bible states God created world and humans.

An asteroid apparently wiped out Dinosaurs,
Theory of evolution claims we were once like apes,
Physics ponders puzzles of the universe and time,
Belief, a sense, the soul imbued with Karmic design.

Reflecting on Death—despair and hope;
Though after being me, I come to naught—
My soul, fiery Phoenix flying the ever-changing sky,
Transient body motionless underground lies.

A Journey

Floating in void, speck of sentience,
"Where am I, what am I?"
Feeling lost, craving physical being,
I make a choice, come to Earth.

Lying in bed, recalling awareness before birth,
Do I dream or was it real experience?
What seems impossible, limited by what we see,
The miracle of our soul in eternal journey.

Hovering, beholding above delivery room,
Swaddled in white wrap, eyes wide open,
A nurse carries the baby to his mother's breast—
Then all goes blank—start of my infancy.

Mom reminiscing, genial nostalgia,
"When you were born your eyes were wide open."
A child, ingenuously, "I remember"—
Puzzled, she takes it as jest.

How our souls emerge from a spiritual source,
Journey to find and claim a body home—mystery.
Craving the feel of sand sifting through our fingers,
Incomplete without staring at, caressing our face.

REMEMBER — REMEMBER — REMEMBER—

Devouring desire to preserve an insight,
The speck trying to carry a memento back,
A souvenir from a foreign land before time.

Passage from cosmic ocean to finite flesh,
Natural return the boundless spiritual realm—
What seems impossible, limited by what we see,
The miracle of our soul in eternal journey.

About the Author

Douglas Gordon Magid, a Queens, New York native, is a retired teacher of English and Creative Writing with a Doctoral degree from St. John's University. The enthusiasm of his students for sharing their creative works has inspired Douglas to put out his own writing. His poems, deeply personal and evocative, often explores life and perspective through imagined voices, aiming to rouse empathy and foster social change.

Now splitting his time between Queens and Puerto Rico, Douglas, along with his wife, enjoys gardening, swimming, nature and travelling. His experiences across cultures have shaped his belief in embracing differences and recognizing commonalities. VOICES YEARNING reflects these diverse influences.

www.ingramcontent.com/pod-product-compliance
Lightning Source LLC
LaVergne TN
LVHW061048070526
838201LV00074B/5221